bare roots

Dear Reader,

A bare root is a plant that adapts to its surroundings and thrives, despite being ripped from its resting place while in a dormant and leafless state. It does not take the old soil with it as it embarks on its new journey, for it has all that it needs to survive within its own body.

Sometimes, life rips us from the places we consider to be solid ground. I hope you find that what you need to survive the conditions of life has been inside you all along.

If you cannot seem to find what you need, perhaps these words can help you reconnect to parts of your soul—parts that need to be left behind, parts you didn't know existed, and parts that are ready to be unearthed, making room for new parts of you to grow.

With courage, hope, and love,

Molly

For the ones
that bury parts
of themselves away

Come and see
the sun again

Contents

I drank,
used drugs,
starved myself,
and sliced my body open,
because I had no idea
how to use my words
How powerful I feel now
By writing my words
rather than speaking them
I have quite literally,
found my voice

Pruning the Damage

These words felt unspeakable
I wrote them down instead

Remember when I was 6
and you punched me in the eye
You thought I'd taken your hat
much to your surprise
The teacher brought you in
and made you apologize
"Sorry" you muttered
but I could see it in your eyes
that you didn't care at all
and you didn't get detention
Just another fighting student
I was given no attention
Though I didn't even do it
I could tell they didn't care
"Boys will be boys," they say
"That's why they pull your hair."

Remember when I was 9
and you gathered the boys in the yard
You made a bet with the group
that getting me to cry wouldn't be hard
You threw rocks in my direction
where they gathered at my feet
You didn't see it then
but I admitted my defeat
Because there were so many of you
A small body of just one was I
A stupid little girl
and all I did was cry

Remember when I was 12
and you called me so many names

"Bucktooth" and "Ugly Rat" were some
that brought me so much shame
But some I didn't understand
"Mosquito-Bite Tits" was one
I thought we were still just kids
and supposed to be having fun
"Why look at my chest anyway?"
I thought, and pondered some
I guess the usual insults
about my crying were done
Now I'm becoming a woman
An exciting time, for the young
In reality, the oppression
had only just begun

Remember when I was 15
and your parents weren't there
We gathered friends and booze
The opportunity was rare
And you suggested we play a game
Strip poker was decided
And though I was uneasy
your eyes said you were excited
And I didn't want to do it
Boys had never seen my body
But you cheered me on competitively
you said I was a "hottie"
You cooed and coaxed and sweet-talked me
though inside I was so afraid
I never thought I'd feel so dirty
My morals were betrayed
Anxious and self-conscious
peer pressure got the best of me

That night I lost my dignity
and what seemed like all the rest of me

Remember when I was 16
and we kissed on the bottom stair
And you told me to follow you
as you caressed my hair
And you saw in my eyes
I was uneasy and afraid
The moment of lust
was beginning to fade
So you made me a promise
"I won't hurt you" you said
"Just tell me to stop,
and we'll slow down instead"
I had no reason to doubt you
I listened to what you said
I trusted your words
as you raped me in bed
And on Monday at school
you mumbled, "I'm sorry"
But like the boy in 1st grade
I didn't buy your story
But boys will be boys
"It was an accident," I said aloud
But I just wanted it to end
because we had drawn a crowd
And everyone thought they knew
what happened that night
I was a slut, you see
because I didn't put up a fight
And they sided with you
because you were such a good guy

And instead of convincing them
all I did was cry

Remember when I was 17
and I went to the party sober
And when I drove you home
you ordered me to pull over
And I knew you were drunk
so I didn't think it was real
When you tried to rape me
I made you a deal
Touch me as much as you want,
for the time being
As long as I got you home
Your house soon we'd be seeing
And I pulled into the driveway
A maniacal smile spread across your face
When I looked in your eyes
you laughed and said,
"This isn't my place."
And I begged you to tell me
which house was yours
I thought I'd be fine
once you opened those car doors
I thought back on the night
and what I did wrong
to give you the idea
I was interested at all
I apologized for mixed signals
It was my fault, I thought
"I didn't mean to lead you on,
in this you had no part"
I thought that'd make things better
and you'd say sorry before you were gone

Instead you called me a bitch
I was the one who was wrong
You slammed the door in my face
and walked up the driveway to go to sleep
Where you slept like a baby
and I didn't sleep a wink
And there that night, tucked into bed
"I deserve this," played on repeat in my head

Mom, remember when I was 18
and came home with blood on my shirt
You gasped and said "What happened?"
It was obvious that I was hurt
I yelled "Nothing happened!"
and that I, of course, was fine
The truth is I don't remember
I was too drunk at that time
I know I let him fuck me
because that was all I could do
There was no use in trying
to explain it to you
My sole mission in life
was to exist only for men
I was hurt once before
It will happen again

And I'm sitting at the bar
too inebriated to care
You slip your hands between my legs
An idea others couldn't bear
Because we hadn't even spoken
or flirted at all
Let's get right to the point

You didn't need to even call
me sweet names, or talk me up nicely
You were entitled to me
We both knew it precisely
Now if I said "No,"
would you have even cared?
Would you have said sorry
if you knew I was scared?
Would you have stopped right then
and there in your tracks?
Or would you have laughed
and told me to relax?
What I didn't know then
was the truth is easy to see
You had no right to touch
me there, obviously
My body is mine, and nobody else's
To protect myself is far from selfish
I wish I was taught that from a young age
"Boys being boys" is not just a stage

Remember in the car
when you whispered to your friend
"Give me three minutes with her,"
a favor he'd extend
Assuming I'd fuck you
because that's what girls do
And I'd be proving the stereotype true
You thought I didn't hear you
You were just being cool
In reality, I heard every word
and you thought I was the fool?

9

How you are my boss
and ask me how I like sex
How you are married
and want my number to text
How you make rape jokes
though you know what I've been through
You don't know it now
but you're just like them too

So many women's stories
are exactly the same
And we sit here
thinking we are to blame
That it's perfectly okay
to be treated this way
When it comes to our bodies
we don't have a say
How about teaching a man
something new
When a woman says no,
she's telling the truth
She's not being flirty, mysterious, or funny
Her name is not "Sweetie"
not "Baby," or "Honey"
Just because she's a woman
doesn't make her incomplete
We are human beings
We're not pieces of meat.

I should have known
smiling at you
was an invitation
to violate me

-Nice Girls Finish Last

March 24th, 2006

Suddenly and violently
I am severed into two
Ruptured by an event
lasting mere minutes
Broken by one act of force,
I am a "before" and "after" story
And I didn't ask
for any of this

His moans, a signal
from that moment on
I am merely a device for gratification
rather than a whole entity
I eventually admit defeat
letting my mind take me away
to a place where I am weightless
and occupying this body
didn't hurt so damn much

I still remember the color and texture
of that ceiling to this day

What happened in
that room was terrible
The aftermath
scarred me more than
I could have ever imagined

You gave me two hours
to do one of the hardest things
I've ever had to do

-"Tell Your Parents"

I would have given anything
for someone,
anyone
to see through the act
and get me help

Mostly,
I think they were all
just relieved
things could go back
to business as usual

I was used to
pulling myself up
by the bootstraps
and plastering
a smile on my face
I became
a professional
that year

To have to pretend
to enjoy the company of your rapist
is not something I ever expect
you to understand

I denied it all
in order to protect him
He was my friend
I make excuses for him
because sometimes
I am afraid
of what will happen
if I tap into the reality
that what he did
was truly unforgivable

He was sorry
asking please,
"Can you not tell
anyone"

I was confused
asking in return,
Isn't it more important
that this doesn't happen again,
to another girl?

His response?
"Kind of."

At least he was honest.

Even though he treated me
like I was nothing but
an empty vessel
and a place to empty
himself into
I still longed for him
I found comfort in this abuse
because
I didn't think
I deserved any better

I started to avoid physical intimacy
Once someone has penetrated you
without your consent
it is hard to let other men be inside you
I started to keep everyone I love at arm's length
Once someone betrays you
and violates you in the most intimate way
it is hard to trust other people again
I stopped interacting with my outside world
because my current world
was filled with trauma and pain
And no matter how eloquently
I speak or write about being raped,
no one will ever understand
what it was like to be violated by you

I walk
speak
think
sleep
and love
differently,
because of you

I Used to Be

I used to be brave
"Fearless," mother called it
Needing no one to teach me
because I could do it on my own
It was endearing when I was young
Because my obstacles, though fairly small
felt like big obstacles to me

I used to be uninhibited
Giggling in awkward ways
Running freely where I went
Stopping only when I lost my breath
and falling down in gasps of laughter

I used to be curious
About life and love and the future
Finding joy in simple things
and soaking up every ounce of experience
this big world had to offer

I used to be nervous
in an innocent way
Wondering if my hair looked okay
what my friends thought of me
and if my grades were good enough
Seeking approval from Mom and Dad
and always wanting to do my best

I used to be unknowing
Not without experimentation
Nonetheless, feeling pure
Pretending to be wiser

I could fool people into thinking
that inside I wasn't still a little girl

I used to be big
Like knowing I was allowed
to take up space in this world
Talking loud and laughing hard
I rightfully took my place
as another spirit on this Earth
And I knew in my heart
that one day maybe,
I could belong

I used to be whole
Some cracking and bruising apparent
Adolescence does that
Yet, every piece of me
still relatively intact
Up until,
that one spring day

And then you came
A devil dressed in blue
Whispering sweet nothings
and promises you couldn't keep
Swallowing my being and
spitting out pieces you didn't need

Disguised as a safety net
A place to go when it's cold
Mocking my stupidity
with every lie you told
Like an auctioneer, within minutes
I was sold

Like a guide dog you lead me
to the last place I felt alive

And.

Then.

I'm.

Suffocated
Crushed beneath the weight
of a thousand words never spoken
A thousand no's never screamed
You break my soul and body
and with every muscle you move,
I stay silent
Every moment that passes
brings you closer to sealing my fate
Your ecstasy, my demise
Every moan of pleasure,
a trowel to my flesh
Digging and jabbing
Pounding and stabbing
Hollowing out a home
for evil to rest forever
long after this excavation has finished

My tarnished skin,
Dirtied
Infected and defiled
My youth permanently soiled

Forever ruined and
contaminated always

And you leave my carcass to rot
like an animal in the wild
The vultures downstairs await
to feed on the spoils
Unaware that a murder most foul
occurred above them while they played

The forced reporting
a violation unto itself
and with every word you speak
of what action I must take,
You are raping me just like he did
all over again

I used to be brave
but now I pretend
Because everyone is watching
and the spotlight is boiling my blood
The sweat above my brow apparent
and the show must go on

I used to be uninhibited
but now I am chained
To a dirty bedroom at a party house
A cemetery of sorts
Visiting in my mind
to pay respect to the girl who once was free
Every movement now, calculated
I don't laugh loud anymore

I used to be curious
about love and life and the future

Hungry for information and
longing to grow up
Now, I am apathetic
Aimlessly dragging myself from place to place
My thoughts shut down
because my mind is now an enemy
My daydreams become nightmares
and my imagination doesn't take me
farther than that bedroom door

I used to be nervous
in an innocent way
But now fear
encompasses my being
And I worry
about safety versus logic
about diseases versus cleanliness
about police and crime
about survival and sanity
The obsessions swirling through my mind
destroying anything in its path
Breaking my shoulders
like an unshakable albatross
The fear,
wraps around my larynx like a boa constrictor
ready to feed on its next kill
and I can't breathe again

I used to be unknowing
Naïve about certain things
that experimenting could not replace
But now, I understand
For I know all that there is to know
About human nature and "love"
about men and trauma

about suffering and pain
about grief and death
about disgust and rage
Not things a young girl should know
I am all too acquainted,
soon growing comfortable
And this agony
will become all I know

I used to be big
Unafraid to take up space in this world
Declaring the world mine to conquer
and explore as I pleased
Now, I am small
Closed off to the world
Averting stares and
dodging conversations
Shrinking my body as though
I may one day disappear with the wind
As insignificant as the dirt
we walk upon each day
Smashed and impacted with each step
Until there's nothing left
but solid, cold, hard ground

I used to be whole
but now, I am broken
Pieces of me scattered
across that dirty bedroom floor
Others struggling to find their place
Their jagged edges smashed together
in a last ditch effort

to keep me alive and intact
Like a broken child's toy
handled too rough
And the evidence,
too hard to conceal

I used to be young
Still finding my way
in this thing we call life
But now, I am old
My body knowing this pain
Aged by brutality
and knowing exactly where I belong
Creases form above my brow
and where my smile should be
Fear encompasses my being
down to my muscles, joints, and bones
Making it hard to move about
freely and carelessly, not stiff
As I do now

And now time has passed
10 years, to be exact
A life of institutions and hospitalizations
Of addictions and attempts
to leave this world and be free
Knowing control of petty things
because you took it from me that night
And I've filled these years
with distractions from your crime

Feeling as though I've lived a thousand lifetimes
Yet am still a young girl inside
Wishing different outcomes
and wasting time thinking what could've been

I take great pleasure
in having a man who treats me well
But what he doesn't know
is that he knows you all his own
The devil inside my soul
He takes us to bed together because,
you never leave
You made your mark back then
that I was yours to own
My scars, a sort of branding
A warning to those who come near
And on those nights he touches me
wanting solely to be with me
I can't help but think back and remember
of how I used to be.

Do I even care
that he hurt me anymore?
Maybe I care
he's happy
and made someone his wife
on my birthday
Mostly,
I'm just angry

I will never be able
to wake up and stop being
a former victim

I will never be able
to conveniently forget
what happened
all those years ago

I will never be able
to unlearn the things I've learned
about the human condition
from these events

Things like this
don't just come with
on and off switches

"Survivor"
felt like a blanket term
I had to call myself
because of course
I was strong
I was capable
I was confident
I was no victim
But deep down
I felt I didn't belong
in this league of women
who fought for their lives
They certainly seemed
a lot braver than I
The only thing
I fought afterwards
was myself

Perhaps it is possible
to be both
survivor and victim
These parts can live
within us simultaneously

-"Both, And"

Why I Don't Seek Support

It is strange
to sit down for coffee
and start discussing something
that happened over a decade ago
and how I'm still struggling
There's just no introduction
for something like that

Trauma
distorts
taints
colors
skews
and manipulates
every situation I come across
I let it leak everywhere
and like a faulty pen
I cannot control the bleeding

I am tired
of seeing your face
everywhere I go

A therapist once told me
I could be triggered
when I give birth
or when my daughter
turns 16 years old
It is then I realize,
this is a lifelong thing

I feel as if I am
avoiding something
just underneath the surface
If I move
I could boil over at any minute
I toss and I turn at night
without knowing the reason why
I can't concentrate
and it hurts all over

-Memories

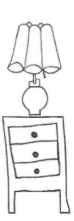

I'm
paralyzed
and
cannot
tell
the past
from
the present
My
throat
is raw
I've
become
a mute
My stare
is glassy
I'm
unresponsive
And like
a 30-year-old
carnival
ride
I'm
shut
down
completely

-"Trauma Land"

PTSD

I have the ability
to travel through time and space
Déjà vu
is not just an eerie feeling
I get every once in a while

Spring

When the snow begins to thaw
and the sun stays out later to play
When the birds start to sing
and tell stories of where they've been
I am not reminded of renewal or hope
Of blooming flowers, or rebirth
Instead, I mourn
I think of disgust and degradation
I think of how I want to disappear
I think of what you did
and how this season changed everything
I beg for cold and rainy days,
praying my mind forgets
I am not granted reprieve
and no matter how hard I try
I cannot seem to reclaim
the spring again

Why I Quit Therapy

I am sick of dredging up old skeletons
that have cemented themselves in my closet
It hurts less that I have them
and more that I try to destroy them
unsuccessfully, time and time again
They've been there so long
the closet is practically
made out of bone

You demonize me
for being used
but not the men
doing the using

-Double Standards

They hate that I was violated
Not for reasons you may think
They fear the loss of credibility
So they question mine

-"The MRA's"

How can I pull the rape card
if the deck was stacked
against me in the first place

In my world
Feelings were not safe
Vulnerability was not safe
Intimacy was not safe
Conflict was not safe
Attention was not safe
Physical touch was not safe
The unknown was not safe
People were not safe
Until one day I realized
the idea of safety in itself,
is all relative

I gave up on
getting justice for myself
a long time ago
Finding closure
was a personal choice

Your role in this timeline changed
You shifted from friend to assailant
within a matter of minutes
You forced your way into this storyline
as a permanent villain,
then added me to your notch post
of unfortunate victims
The fairy tale turned dark quickly
and you have only yourself to blame
The good news is that
you were only a chapter of my story,
which has yet to be finished
Spoiler alert:
I am the heroine of this narrative

-"Rewrite"

Over time, as the trauma compounded
I learned that surviving is easy
It's the living part that's hard.

Battling the Weeds

I had a nightmare
the Universe swallowed me whole
And as I lay on the cool, dark Earth,
vines split the ground beneath me
Forcefully binding my wrists
and wrapping themselves around me
These malevolent tendrils
angrily vowed to keep me tethered,
despite my own desires to be free
I coughed and I gagged
and as my own body engaged in this battle,
a garter snake made its way up my windpipe
Its scales scraping along my trachea
with every painful movement
The vines, still restricting me
I thrash and I grab,
but my choking doesn't cease

When I wake up from this nightmare
I realize,
I wasn't sleeping at all
The vines were restraints
The garter snake, a breathing tube
And I am still part
of this Universe
after all

She said to me softly
What has your body
ever done to you?
I thought
How has having this body
ever helped me before?

The more of me there is,
the more of me you taunt
Everyone knows I am better
when there is less of me

I hated
taking up so much space
I hated
my curves
I hated
being loud
obnoxious
and imperfect
You promised me
everything I wasn't
To be quiet
shrinking
and invisible

-"E.D."

Stop commenting on this body
It has been through too much already

Restoring the weight
made people assume
I was cured
I was happy
I was healthy

I'm glad the idea
that my body speaks for me
more than my words do
is still true
It's not like I spent months
abandoning that notion
anyway

Collarbones Are Romantic

Reminiscing
about getting sick again
is just deadly sentimentality
Oh,
how I long to be
fragile again

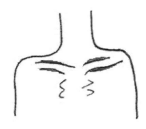

With every relapse
came painful lessons
I didn't want to learn
again

I feared you'd think weakness of me
I gave in to the demons again
I felt you'd judge me,
finally seeing me for
what I knew I truly was
A fraud

-"Slipping"

People think "Ana"
just suddenly goes away
The best I got
was to get her
to be a quiet whisper
rather than
an overpowering scream

Dear Eating Disorder,

I miss feeling fragile
and safe with you
Like I was protected,
and no one could touch me
It was you and me until the end,
and nothing else mattered
I miss being just out of people's grasp
because if I was just out of their grasp,
they couldn't possibly hurt me

I miss feeling productive
24 hours of the day with you
I was so hungry, anxious,
and starving all I did
was run errands all day
There couldn't possibly be
time for anything else

I miss feeling like Superwoman with you
I could defy hunger cues and
basic physiological needs,
yet still carry on
I was stronger than everyone else
because I knew how to
control
control
control

But there are things
I will never, ever
miss about you

You made me cold
Not just physically
like I had no circulation
in my toes or fingers
But like my soul was cold,
unreachable, and drained
I felt I only existed on this Earth
to count calories, exercise,
and lose weight

You made me dumb
Not just dumb
like making poor decisions
about my health and my well-being
But dumb like I couldn't even
form sentences
I was so damn hungry
All I needed was some fat
or protein in my diet

You made me afraid
Not just afraid of calories,
sugar, fat, and food
But of love
I was afraid to love and be loved
I was afraid to be touch and be touched
I was afraid of others but mostly,
I was afraid of myself

You ripped my heart
right out of my chest
The beat of it was nothing but
a solid, empty drum
taunting and reminding me
I am still on this Earth
despite my own wishes to be
anywhere but in the present moment

You lied to me
You said I would feel better
when I was thin, small, and non-existent
You made "beautiful" and
"emaciated" synonymous
You ruptured my entire sense of self

You said people would like me better
when I was quieter and shrinking
When I took up less space in this world
In reality, you turned a vibrant young woman
into an obsessive, fearful, selfish little girl
People who once were drawn to her
saw her disappear into the background

You got what you wanted
for a short time,
but it did not last
I have succeeded in spite of you, old friend
My light may have been dimmed
by your icy, overbearing presence,
but it has never gone out

Longing for you
does not make me weak
Being able to stay away from you
despite your own plans
is what makes me strong

Dear eating disorder,
I call the shots
forever and always
Do your best
I will not falter.

It seems as though
I am so allergic to my own emotions
I truly believe I can permanently run from them
without them
        catching
             up
               to
                 me.

Self-sabotage
is my biggest weakness
and my favorite vice

I have not lived without
an emotional crutch
since I was thirteen years old

I remember the pain afterwards
The *real* pain
The stinging showers
the gasps when I bumped it the wrong way
the awkward sleeping positions
and the excuses I made,
about where the injuries came from
The multiple infections
the antibiotic ointments
the endless supply of bandages
and the makeup I applied,
even though it never look quite right
The kit of weapons
The itchy scabs
The nasty scars
and the disappointment and sadness
on my loved ones' faces,
when they finally figured it out
The belly full of sick secrets
and the eternal shame in knowing,
I get a sick pleasure
out of torturing myself
I remember it all
It is impossible to forget,
because my scars will never let me

The booze is hard to quit
For once,
I stopped giving a shit
about the house being spotless
my body being perfect
and whether or not I was smiling

I'm terrified
to be in my own body
and feel things
I don't know
that I can handle alone

I'm afraid to discover
that life is rather ordinary, after all
That my destiny is simply
to roam this Earth,
aimlessly searching for meaning,
and die before I ever feel
truly fulfilled or at peace

Writer's Block

My thoughts submerged
in heavy waters
of self-centeredness
Tied to cinder blocks
of desperation
Sinking and
unable to be located
I swim towards the top
of shallow expressions
My syntax running away with the tides
Flowing far outside my reach
I grasp for the right words
that I cannot seem to find

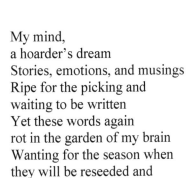

My mind,
a hoarder's dream
Stories, emotions, and musings
Ripe for the picking and
waiting to be written
Yet these words again
rot in the garden of my brain
Wanting for the season when
they will be reseeded and
flourish once again

I sift through the happenings
attempting to pick gems from the lot
I drive along the highway
wishing for the horizon
Yet all I can do
is see five feet in front of me

The ideas I write on the mirror
disappear in the steam

My notions resemble butterflies
Not for their beauty, rather
their lack of permanence
A quick flash upon a flower
A hasty streak of beauty
When I try to seize them
eager to connect if only,
for a moment
I blink in distraction and
they are gone again

Depression
is not a phase
It is not
a mild case of the blues
that a little jogging can fix

People with depression
are silently imploding
They are stifled by their fears,
their thoughts,
and the voice that tells them
they will never be good enough
They are often exceptionally
intelligent and bright people
It wears many masks and
lives within many good people
Please,
tell your loved ones
they matter

I fooled myself into thinking
if I just kept smiling and faking it
the all-encompassing despair
and the overwhelming sadness
would eventually just fade away
I became sicker and farther from help
with every "I'm fine," I spewed

-The Repercussions of Depression

I felt so tired
I could barely function
and so guilty
I didn't have more energy
The contradiction
was not lost on me
but was crippling
nonetheless

I needed help
but had a lifetime
of willful independence
to undo

I was stuck
between two false worlds
Versions of myself I created
in order to fool and protect
In reality
I was neither person
I was a ghost

The idea that suicide is an option
was like a demon, always on my shoulder
The anguish and logic permanently
competing for center stage
The trauma, the addiction,
and the pain seemed too much to bear
I felt I didn't belong here,
chained to this Earth
full of so much suffering
I was too sensitive and fragile for this world
People hurt me,
almost as much as I hurt myself
When you live with this monster for so long
the thought of leaving can become
somewhat of an obsession
Like a constant companion
it reassured me
that no matter how bad things became,
there was always a way out of this

Some people say
they met God
or felt peace during
their near-death experience
I think part of me
just wanted to see
if they were lying or not

My heart pounded
with a vigorous desperation
as if trying to free itself
from my chest cavity
I couldn't tell if it was
nervousness,
the pills,
or the sheer thrill
that it would all be over soon
I closed my eyes
and found comfort in the soft music
I waited for the
sweet release of death
to carry me away,
but it never came
My biggest failure
is now my greatest blessing

I was confined to a hospital bed
Barely alive, dysfunctional,
and supported by machines
Dependent on strangers
to ensure my survival
The severity of my situation
took several days to comprehend
The repercussions of my choices delayed
as I existed in a dream-like fog
I floated between life and death and
unceasingly questioned my circumstances
on repeat

Maybe the gravity of it all
took so long to understand
because a vast part of me
felt utter relief
Throughout my short life
I consistently felt the weight
of the disparity between
how I felt on the inside
and how I looked on the outside
I hate to admit that things
felt a little more congruent
after this

Blue lips and low O_2
The cord wrapped around my neck
A pair of headphones,
I wasn't supposed to have
I remember the screams
I'm going to touch you now
and multiple staff restraints
Strapping me to a gurney
just like they do in the movies
Wheeling me to a dark room
with dimly a lit spotlight
I lay flat out on the table
still strapped down at the wrists
Feeling much like a prisoner
awaiting my execution
I stared at the ceiling
Multiple authority figures
interrogated a silent, sullen body
Judge and jury decided
The verdict was in
A night in isolation as punishment
I sure as hell
never tried that again

I stopped counting
the number of respected institutions
that reprimanded me, shamed me,
or simply kicked me out
for harming myself upon their watch
This sin apparently graver than any other
The places I sought out
to provide aid and support me
even now saw my problems
as mere liabilities
How can one go on
without finally giving in
to the belief that they are
hopeless and an infinite burden?
The message could not
have been clearer
I was a lost cause
and a problem,
unable to be solved

This place is not for you
I heard over and over
for simply wearing my self-hate
on my sleeve, quite literally
I knew I should have just kept quiet
about my aversion to myself
just like everybody else does

Stop diagnosing me
and feeding me pills
Instead of sitting down
and talking to me
like I'm a human being
Not some caged zoo animal
you like to experiment on

- *Psychiatry*

Isolation

A padded room
too extravagant for my error
Rather, a utility closet
seemed fitting to both parties
Walls and floors of concrete
I was given a blanket
and small pillow, sans case

I should have known better
than to hurt myself within
a contained environment
Didn't I know, they could
hurt me even worse?
Humiliation and degradation
cut way deeper
than razors do

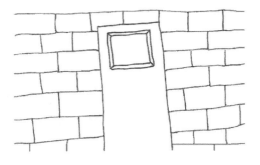

The Truth About Psych Wards

They don't hold you down
and inject you with tranquilizers
That would be barbaric, at best
What they do instead
is dangle their power,
exert their authority,
and maintain their dominance
by offering you "choices"
Crying in your room all day?
"Choose" to take the pill
or "force us" to use the needle
The manipulation of the language
making it seem so much softer,
and allowing them to sleep at night
Justifying their oversights,
they maintain the lie they tell themselves
that they are saving our poor, lost souls
We just want to help you, meaning
We just don't have time for you,
and so I become a docile, little lamb

Why talk to me
when you can just
treat me like a statistic?
Numbers are less complex
than people anyway

The Roses (and the Thorns)

Perhaps the scariest part of all
is admitting that the person
we loved for so long
may not be the person
we thought they were at all
That you can know so little
about someone who you've shared
intricate intimacies with for weeks,
months, or even years
The what-ifs can
easily poison the mind

I know what it's like
to be left desperately confused
The unanswered questions
gnawing at every fiber of your being
Keeping you awake at night
and leaving you exhausted in the morning
How did this happen so quickly?
How could he do this to me?
And why pull me in so tight
just to rip the blanket out
from underneath me?
The truth is that
he was human and
like I, imperfect
We both made mistakes
Mistakes that neither of us
were ever able to recover from

Fools Rush In

To others
it may have just seemed like
teenage puppy-love
A doomed relationship
so inappropriately intense
for our maturity level
But it changed me

The reason we met
and the Universe's purpose for us
may not have been what I wanted at the time
but it taught me a great deal in the long run
I couldn't see that then

-Lessons from Heartbreak

Sometimes
we want so badly
to believe the good in people
we ignore our gut instincts
Optimism shouldn't be
such a fatal flaw

If I pretend to be
someone better, stronger,
or tougher than who I really am
you can never really hurt or break me
The person you think you are hurting
technically does not exist

-Defense Mechanisms

Giving unwarranted faith to others
has made me vulnerable before
Yet always being skeptical of others' intentions
has made me rather hard-hearted and closed off
I don't know which one I'd rather be
Both methods of being bring me immense pain

I wonder if anyone else
feels overwhelming loneliness
even when they are surrounded
by people all the time

Be like a duck in water
they patronize
Let it roll off your back
they condescend
Go with the flow more
they squawk
Draping these sentiments
in fabricated concern
Hiding their lack of patience
and revealing the cold, hard truth
Their belief that sensitivity
is equal to burdensome
and really, just
an inconvenience in general

I've wasted my entire life
trying to change this
unsavory part of my psyche
Proving fruitless, every time
Feeling so intensely
may be my biggest curse
but it is also my favorite blessing
And fuck you
for trying to mold me
into quiet compliancy

There were so many things
I didn't want you to know
There are still so many things
I'm afraid for you to know

The wedding was beautiful
and everything I dreamed of
But it didn't fix me
What now?

-"The Honeymoon's Over"

I don't know how you were able
to think clearly during those times
and how you survived it
but you did
We did.

We bought a new home
A new space, a new life
One of love and light
away from all the memories
I know we'll get there
It just takes time

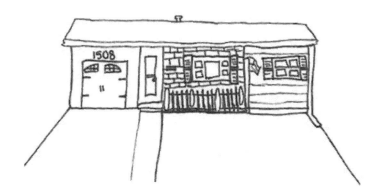

The vacuum
drowns out the
intolerable noise
The deafening silence,
of things we never dare
speak aloud

-"Chores"

Oblivion

Your rosy cheeks
Your dozy eyes
Stealing a glance
becomes a longing stare
Soaked with motives,
I know all too well

Your expression,
A familiar face
I cannot deny
A drunk man
in my sacred space
The homeliness of your soul
becomes a blackened abyss
Your fingers are daggers
My body,
barbed wire

You,
A stranger within these barricades
And I prefer the cordiality
where interactions are safe
within the walls of sobriety

But this bottle we covet
Now secret elixir

The warm coat we wear
to soften the edges of the pain

Glass after glass
I feel numbness at last
My shoulders relax
and I can breathe again

When terror comes knocking
the answer becomes clear
Pour another one dear
And again,
oblivion

I push you away
I have trained myself well
And you
as my student
let me do it
every
single
time

-"Teacher"

You see flickers
of the old me
come back sometimes
I need you to know
for the most part
that girl is gone

-"Gone Girl"

Loving me
takes work sometimes
but you never complain
Most days
I don't know what I did
to deserve you

I want to stop this cycle
of self-destruction
If I have learned anything,
it is that I'm not just
hurting myself anymore
I'm hurting you, too

-"For Us"

I know my words
don't always align with my actions
You hear me say *I love you,*
but you see me shrink in your presence
It's probably easy
to question my love for you
on most days

-It's Not You, It's Me

I am sorry
you constantly pay the price
for other men's mistakes
It is okay to be angry
I understand
you didn't sign up
for any of this

I asked him to describe me

in one, solitary word:

"Fiery," he said.

What could I say?

"I am a Leo, after all"

-Date Night

The hardest part
of meeting the love of your life
when you're 20
is growing into different people
and being forced to decide
if that love is workable
or even relatively the same
when you're 30

-"We've Changed"

We don't talk about it
Yet some days
it feels like the center of our worlds
I've been waiting for
the elephant in the room
to disappear for so long
but it just doesn't
really go anywhere
I've realized
we are both numb to it
We have learned
to ignore its' company
I can't decide whether to be
relieved or ashamed

-The Elephant in the Bedroom

It is incomprehensible,
the idea that other people
love me unconditionally
Sometimes I find myself
resenting them the most
I can't seem to let them in
no matter how hard I try
Their presence only reminds me
how damaged I truly am

I spend most of my time
pushing other people away
with the hopes of peace,
simplicity, and solitude
Yet when I finally achieve this goal
all I feel is insurmountable emptiness,
loneliness, and despair

-"Push, Pull"

Words don't fix me
and certain words really hurt me
I don't need to be told
that this will pass
that I need to cheer up
or that I need be anything other
than how I am
in this exact moment

-*How to Love Me*

Connection

I crave it and
I seek it out
I'm drawn in
like a moth to a flame
Yet as I draw closer,
I recoil from the heat
It is everything I want
and everything I fear
all at the same time

Consistently trying to fix me
reinforces the idea that I'm broken

I'm

                not

                        broken.

Empathy doesn't always
come in the form of soft words,
coated with warm
and fuzzy sentiments
Expressing rage
can be empathetic too

Introvert

Don't get me wrong
I love people
But mostly,
they suck up my energy
like a high-powered vacuum

Adults are weird
We can't make friends
like we used to when we were little
We need to do more research first

It's a beautiful thing
when two individuals
can be present for each other's
struggles and pain
with no expectations attached
I am better for knowing you

-To My Friends Near and Far

When I feel heard
understood
and loved,
When I really let it sink in
and wrap its arms around me,
When I soak in its warmth
like a hot bath,
It is way better than
any addiction or high
could ever give me

Good friends show concern,
but know when to trust you
and when to let you
have your whole experience
After they've given their two cents
and told you they care about you,
they don't try to fix it
Rather they agree solely,
to be a silent passenger
A witness, on this ride
They make space for your pain
if and when you need it,
and may even agree to hold it
for a little while, when you cannot
They may sometimes disagree
with the way you handle your pain,
but they will never, ever
turn their back on you

We didn't choose to be
strung together
by the thread of trauma
Yet here we are
People who have been wounded,
clawed their way out of the
depths of darkness,
and managed to survive and thrive
We all deserve love, respect,
and kindness
Things we never had
when we were abused

-"Nasty Women"

Ode to Pearl

My emotional support dog
A gift, from the shelter
You are one anxious pup
and though I spend
a lot of time supporting you,
it is still pretty clear to me
who rescued who

The Seedling Shall Blossom

I remember every time
a woman criticized or shamed me
for my hunger
my clumsiness
my loudness
and being anything other than small and lady-like
The insults disguised as questions
like *Are you going to eat all that?*
The seemingly meaningless gestures
like a gentle belly-pat during puberty
The demands soaked in disapproval
like ensuring I didn't gain the weight back,
wishing I wore more feminine clothes,
and telling me I swear too much
Then finally,
the aching contradictions
Rendering me hopeless and confused
You're too skinny now!
In my heart, I finally accepted
I'd never be good enough for them
I would always be too *something*
as a woman, failing to live up
to their outdated expectations
I regained power when I decided
this was less about me,
and how they judged me
and more about them,
and how they judged themselves
and internalizing the opinions
of the critical women from their childhoods
is not my cross to bear

Stroking my arm, she jokingly asked if tattoos rub off
She was positive I'd regret it in 10 years' time

*Do you want to make a bet
that I will still love it in 10 years?*

"No, no…"

Why not?

"I'll probably be dead by then."

-Grandma

Being the youngest child
and lone female of the bunch
was at times, a thankless job
I grew weary as the years passed
because it was always my job
to be dainty and appealing,
and to be everybody's play thing
As I matured I realized
this wasn't who I wanted to be at all
I wasted so many years
playing that role

Crybaby

Ever since I could remember
my eyes would never stop leaking
My constant emotional episodes
always embarrassing me, never ceasing
It happened to me time and time again
my spirit kept on breaking
Until one day I promised myself
I'd be the best at faking
I'd hide my tears from family
I'd hide my tears from friends
I'd be the strongest girl there was
they'd all owe me amends
And now years later, far from it all
tears should be safe to show
But you see, I once was a crybaby
and I never want you to know

They say words
can never hurt you
*I'll take sticks and stones
any day of the week*

You told me
to get thicker skin
so I took my pain
and traded it
for an impenetrable shell

Being a *nice girl*
was surviving a war
My voice and concerns often silenced,
stifled, or mocked in some way
That is, if I actually
worked up the courage
to even speak at all
Over time I simply stopped
trying to use my words
I spoke with self-violence instead

Conflict
was a completely
foreign concept to me
A positive spin
and a slight sugar-coating
never hurt anyone,
right?

Problems
were to be dealt with quietly
and protecting me
was less important
than teaching me passivity

I thought
I infinitely owed the world
and the people in it
every last piece of me
It wasn't hard
to give these pieces away
when I felt broken
to begin with

If I had a superpower
I'd tell you it was invisibility
I can hide from anyone in plain sight
My smile is my mask
My baggy, boring clothes
provide me a costume
I feed you happy lies
This, is my shield

Why color outside the lines
when it's perfectly safe inside them
Lines were made for a reason

By refusing to engage with others,
I'm missing out on possible
opportunities for connection

By dumbing down my appearance,
I'm denying myself the right
to feel confident in my own skin

By rejecting physical touch,
I'm losing the ability to feel loved
and cared for

Acting like a robot
may be safe and predictable,
but it's also lonely
and mind-numbingly boring

Sometimes
attempting to operate as
a strong woman in this world
is terrifying
Sometimes
all I want to do
is crawl back
into my safe bubble
where at least I know
where I belong:
At the bottom

Superwoman

On the outside
you see Superwoman
What you don't know
is once you rip her mask away,
she is not safe
Inside her body
lives a terrified little girl
Her skin is as thin as paper
and her mind is full of fear
She still believes in good things,
but she is quick to fall apart
This girl cannot be a part
of this world right now
She is not strong enough

Superwoman takes the reigns
and you all know no different
You are happy to know
this version of her
because she is strong,
confident, and capable
She is not fragile,
needy, or helpless
Things she truly feels
she is on the inside

When will I stop apologizing
for merely existing?

My lack of self-esteem
is a bad virus that
follows me around
The symptoms flare up
from time to time
but lay dormant
in my system
indefinitely

-Self-Hate is a Sickness

Sometimes I think
about my friends,
my students,
and my future daughter
Would I ever want them
to starve
to bleed
to poison themselves
and to treat their body
like it's disposable,
wishing pain upon it
every single day?
Sometimes I think
about how I am a friend,
I was a student,
and I am a daughter
And I don't think they
would ever wish any
of those things upon me

Teaching little girls
to constantly smile
to bat their eyelashes
and not make waves
is damaging
Girls like this grow up
not knowing that saying no
is even an option

We need to be coy
yet still know how to protect ourselves
We need to act vulnerable
but not actually put our bodies in harm's way
We need to be feminine
but still know how to hang with the boys
I know we expect a lot from men
But at least they aren't conflicting roles

-Living Contradictions

Being a people-pleaser
is like being a smoker
It's easy to become one
when you're surrounded by them
It costs you a lot
whether emotionally or financially
It gives you a high
when you concede to its' demands
And it seems impossible to quit
when it is all you've known for years

How do I just stop
caring about what other people think?
I don't know any other way
of existing in this world

-*When You Care Too Much*

Why am I not achieving?
Why am I not productive?
Why am I not smaller?
Why am I not better?
Why am I so annoying?
Why am I so needy?
Why do I cry so much?
These questions
are flesh-eating bacteria,
gnawing at my soul
night after night
I toss and turn endlessly
without answers
coming up empty-handed
every morning

The "should's"
are overwhelming
I wish I could erase
the rulebook
inside my mind

I was never taught
it's okay to be tough
I was never taught
it's okay to defend myself
I was never taught
it's okay to tell vile men
to get off my body
We need to do right
by this next generation of women
Teaching them
these things don't just come
with the territory of being female
They don't have to believe the lie
that suffering in silence
is their only option,
as many of us have done
for the majority of our lives

If I ever have a daughter
my wish for her
is that she is strong,
independent,
and learns to value
her own sense of security
before anyone's feelings
without apologizing for any of it
And if she is more like me
and needs support in this area,
that's okay, too

When the crumbly
12-year-old me chimes in
about how I am not good enough
or how I am less than perfect
I tell her to pipe down
Adult me has it under control

I am slowly learning
how to stand up for myself
I have spent too many years
ignoring my gut instinct
and living in fear
Staying quiet and lending respect
to undeserving people
has gotten me nowhere,
my entire life
If the only way
my message is received
is with venom and rage
I'm okay with that
I'm taking care of me now

-I'm Done Playing Nice

Sometimes
in order to get our point across
we need to roar the loudest
There is nothing wrong
with ruffling a few feathers
while trying to discover
your inner beast

The Anthem of the Privileged

It doesn't affect me
Why should I do
anything about it?

Love Trumps Hate

These headlines
swirl around my mind as
tapeworms
Devouring my thoughts and
feeding off my soul
I feel as if I am in a movie
A world made only for the screen
We are all falling apart,
simultaneously
What can I do?
Sometimes, it is merely
not allowing the anger
and helplessness
to fully consume me

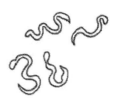

I'm incredibly tired
of people acting like men
are these fucking baboons
that don't understand
when no means no
That we need to hold their hand
and teach them about manners,
personal boundaries,
and a bunch of shit
you literally learn
in elementary school
It's insulting to victims
and to all the men out there
that respect women enough
to actually listen to them

We don't want you to ask intrusive questions
We don't want you to make it about you
We don't want looks of disgust, pity, or shame
We don't want you to start talking about
prevention tactics, or talk about what we
should have done differently
For God's sake,
we just want to feel heard and understood
Something we weren't granted
when we were violated in the first place

-*When We Trust You Enough To Tell You*

In addition to
educating ourselves,
avoiding danger,
and being willing to take responsibility
for being taken advantage of,
we are now responsible for
educating and sympathizing
with perpetrators, too?
For a society that tends to
view women as less-than,
we sure are giving them
a lot of power and responsibility

My throat is raw
from shouting these things
from the rooftops
over and over and over

When I was younger
I couldn't show up for myself
Now that I am an adult
I have a choice
in how I make up
for lost time

-"Choices"

Cultivating Wisdom

There are two absolutes
in this life
We are born on this Earth
and we die on this Earth
The rest of it?
The space between it all?
Is up to us

In a world of stunted emotions
and a world of distractions
We're driven by achievements
and competitions alike
Schedules full,
hearts empty
Our time
slips through the hourglass
over and over again

-"Hourglass"

We are afraid of the truth,
and we are afraid of ourselves
We are afraid the people we love
will leave us, if they know who we really are
We are afraid we will never be good enough,
or live up to expectations
We are afraid of living an unfulfilled life,
yet we are afraid to die
Our worlds are quiet contradictions
and we can't quite make sense of it all,
so we just *do* things instead

-"Fear Keeps Us Busy"

We want to prove we are in pain
and that the pain has meaning
We start to use our self-destructive behaviors
to speak for us, in hopes that
we won't have to say those words aloud:
The truth
We start to exchange war stories like currency
Unknowingly engaging in silent competitions
to see who is suffering the most
Except nobody wins here
We start to bury our suffering
and center our conversations around
our diagnoses, labels,
and masochistic tendencies
This is the way we hide
from our true selves

We spend our days
manipulating,
controlling,
crunching time,
and making plans
In the presence of it all,
we forget to breathe
Just breathe.

Sometimes
it is okay
to sit in silence
We can feel and learn
just as much
in moments
of quiet solitude
and peace

Sometimes
the toughest exteriors
are home to the most
fragile souls

-"Armored"

Growth is painful
In order to stay
a work in progress
you must welcome the pain
with open arms
If I have learned anything,
it is that you will
feel the pain regardless
of whether you fight it or not
Life has its own plans

-"Growing Pains"

There are no good years or bad years
A year is just a string of 365 days
that we give a whole lot of meaning to
I don't know if I will be happier,
healthier, or better next year
But I do know one thing
I will be wiser

-Measuring The Years

What They Don't Tell You In College

What they don't tell you in college
is that your job may not fulfill you
or be the reason you get out of bed every day
You may never find that "dream gig"
or make $100,000 a year

What they don't tell you in college
is that it is okay to settle in your career
because a paycheck is really,
just a piece of paper
and your resume isn't
a permanent ticket out of suffering

What they don't tell you in college
is that all you need to survive life as an adult
is find a passion and a reason
to keep living through the bullshit
like when you can't pay your bills,
and you have no idea what
you are doing with your life

What they don't tell you in college
is that maybe your job does
make you feel satisfied and complete,
but there is a good chance
it could be something else
And it is okay to change your mind

What they don't tell you in college
is that adults are just giant children,
trying to figure it out like the rest of us
and that they don't actually have all the answers
as we've always been led to believe

What they don't tell you in college
is that you will probably never feel
like you fully have your shit together
and what they fail to mention is that
there is nothing wrong
with you because of it

The double-edged sword
of being a grown up
is being able to do
anything you want
but not having time to do
anything at all

My addictions
served many purposes
One very simple one being,
they filled my time
What now?

-Bored

People always told me
things would get better with age
I'm starting to believe them
I'm a lot lazier with my
self-destruction these days

- Epiphanies From my Late Twenties

The Definition of Suffering

Confusing things I can't control
with things that I can

I am not the type of person
to let things go
and I never will be
I can only learn
how to deal with the pain
more gracefully
and self-soothe
more effectively

-Know Thyself

It is not my fault
the world was so ill-prepared
for people who feel
as deeply as I do

-Unburdening

There were many times
I never wanted another birthday
I didn't think I deserved
to take up space on this planet
Today, I am glad I can still say
"It's my birthday."
Whether that day is awesome,
boring, traumatic, or regular,
It still exists
and I am here to experience it
So here's to more of these weird days,
where we receive gifts just for being born
[And here's to more crying on them, too]

-"It's My Birthday & I'll Cry if I Want To"

I think it is relatively normal
for people to question their existence
Maybe even fantasizing
about suicide, at times
Life has little meaning
if you don't question it
every once in a while
The uncertainty proving,
you care about your purpose
and respect the gravity
of being given a life at all

There is a purpose to our suffering
Only when I look back am I able to
appreciate the struggle for what it was
and recognize that it led me to exactly
where I needed to be today
What a relief to give in
to the Universe's grand plan
Knowing in my heart
things always work out
the way they are supposed to
even though I may fight them
in the moment

-Trusting the Process

Ignorance may be bliss
but it's a shallow way of life
I'll take complexity and struggle
any day of the week
After years of anguish
I appreciate the fact
that wisdom is a gift
not afforded to all

To Thrive

My goal is this life
is to blossom and fly
Jump leaps and bounds
let my dreams touch the sky
For once in my life
I want to feel fully alive
Not just do what I do best
and merely survive

Buds of Hope

Keep Going

When you are exhausted from crying all day,
and think it will never stop

When the most you can do is let your dog out,
only to fall back into a listless, fitful sleep

When you're convinced they'd be better off without
you, and that you're merely a burden to others

When you think there is nothing to live for,
and hope is fleeting

When you feel numb because you've been sad for so long,
and you simply cannot stand it any longer

On the days you hate yourself for always feeling like this,
yet you feel helpless to change it at all

When you wonder what it's all for,
and can't find reasons to stay alive

When all you can think about is leaving this earth,
and finally feeling peace at last

When your body feels more foreign than the space you
occupy, and you don't understand why

When the nightmares are rampant,
and the insomnia is too powerful to overcome

When you believe we are solely on this earth to suffer,
and it's unfair and unfathomable

When you feel so alone in this world, even when
surrounded by friends and family that love you the most

On your darkest days
even if it's a baby step, a trudge,
or simply not sliding backwards
into the abyss,

Just.

Keep.

Going.

Recovery
feels like you're dying for a little bit
But what follows
is an incredible high
You feel like you are flying
and completely free
like a blank canvas,
just waiting to be created

It can be quite frightening
to admit to yourself
just how powerful you are
Your presence,
a spotlight in a darkened room
Your strength,
enough to move mountains
Your beauty,
as rich as a sunset in June
Your soul,
as brilliant as a woven tapestry
Your hope,
an inextinguishable flame
And your love,
as perfectly complex as you are
Don't forget that you
are a gift to this world,
and to the people who want
nothing more
than just to have you in it

To the Person on the Verge of Relapse

I know you're tired
and fighting feels exhausting
You feel like you're losing
an uphill battle

I know that falling back into the numbers
and the thin, clean lines of life
seems enticing because
life is so damn complicated
and scary sometimes
The calories, the weight,
and the nothingness
seem so much safer right now

I know the itchy, tingly feeling
on your body and in your brain
Like you want to unzip your skin
and crawl out, and it feels as though
nothing will fix that feeling
until you get that substance in your body
and can finally breathe a sigh of relief

I know how badly
you want to pick up that weapon
and use it on yourself
The self-destructive urges
feel too incredible to handle
and when they come,
It feels like a wave encompasses
your entire being

In a few minutes you know,
you will feel calm
and okay with the world

I also know,
none of these things hold the answer
to your current dilemma
And none of this should come
at your body's expense,
dear friend

Getting through to the other side
is worth it, so much that
maybe someday
you can help someone else
who is struggling, too
Just hang on a little longer,
please

Recovery
isn't about having
an undefeated season
It's about winning
the fights
that mean the most

Helping others isn't always being
a shining role model
Sometimes
it is showing people
that you are human
Flawed,
scarred,
but *alive*

Free yourself
from the bondage of rules and rituals
Let go
of the things that aren't just right or perfect
Relax
because you deserve it
Take risks
even though it may be terrifying
Be vulnerable
instead of running to the other room to cry
And stand tall
because you can do strong all on your own

-You Got This

Be kind to yourself
Nurture the part of you
that needs to be loved
and let the Universe do the rest
You deserve a break
every once in a while

Recovery isn't planning the day
you will let go or fully surrender
It's just doing it
Now, later today, tomorrow,
and every day after that

Never.

Stop.

Surrendering.

You are not
broken,
defective,
abnormal,
or wrong
We are all just
deeply wounded creatures
doing our best to heal
and find our way in this world

I want to give a voice
to the people who live with
the obsession to leave this world
You are not alone,
and there is no shame
in your existential struggle

You'll Be Okay

I know words don't fix it
so it may sound trite
when I say that
I am really sorry
but I am
Heartache like this
is the worst feeling
You'll be okay
Maybe not now
But soon,
I promise

I hope the intensity
of the memories
slow down,
and haunt you
less and less
with each passing day

There is hope
It may feel like big dreams
and bright skies
or it may feel like the sunlight
barely breaking through the clouds
on a dreary day
It doesn't matter what it looks like
What matters is that you find it
and never let it go

Things aren't perfect
but they are manageable
Don't give up
It gets better

Congratulations
on making it through another tough day
I wish you complexity and discovery
throughout the rest of your days
as you walk, march,
or crawl your way through
this weird thing we call life

Give yourself credit
for all of the hard work you have done
and all the hard work you will continue to do
And when you feel like you aren't worth it
You can come back and reread this
whenever you need it

-You Are Loved

65289165R00128

Made in the USA
Middletown, DE
24 February 2018